BK 923.273 M146M
MCGOVERN: THE MAN
1972
3000 285717 30018
St. Louis Community College
W9-DJE-526

# McGOVERN: The Man and His Beliefs

# McGOVERN
# THE MAN AND HIS BELIEFS

*Selected and Edited*

By SHIRLEY MacLAINE

W • W • NORTON & COMPANY • INC •
NEW YORK

Library of Congress Cataloging in Publication Data

McGovern, George Stanley, 1922–
McGovern: the man and his beliefs.

I. MacLaine, Shirley, 1934– ed.
II. Title.
E840.8.M34A25 1972 328.73'092'4 [B] 72-6760
ISBN 0-393-05341-5



Published simultaneously in Canada
by George J. McLeod Limited, Toronto

PRINTED IN THE UNITED STATES OF AMERICA

1 2 3 4 5 6 7 8 9 0

# McGOVERN: The Man and His Beliefs

# The Man and His Beliefs

**I pledge to seek and speak the truth with all the resources of mind and spirit I command.**

N.Y. POST—ARTIE POMERANTZ

N.Y. POST—VERNON SHIBLA

America is not an establishment. It is not even a government or a constitution. It is a process.

WIDE WORLD

WIDE WORLD

To remain silent in the face of policies that one believes to be hurting the nation is not patriotism, but moral cowardice.

True loyalty is the realization that this country was born in revolution, nurtured in protest, and strengthened by dissent.

Dissent is not just something we can live with; it is something we cannot live without. It is not only consistent with patriotism; it is the highest patriotism.

We must recognize that it is not nearly so helpful to do things for people as it is to create the conditions in which people can do things for themselves.

I would pledge that I will never advocate a course in private that I am ashamed to defend in public.

How can you represent a people if you don't know what's on their minds?

The President of the United States can restore respect for truth. He can renew this country's commitment to justice, and he can find the compassion and decency that also live in each American. And that is the search I want to make.

N.Y. POST—BARNEY STEIN

N.Y. POST—BARNEY STEIN

No single nation has the power, the wisdom, or the mission to be the world's policeman, banker, or judge. These are the functions of the agencies of the international community.

WIDE WORLD

## War

I'm fed up with old men dreaming up wars for young men to die in.

WIDE WORLD

JILL KREMENTZ

Ours is a generation under pressure, engaged in a struggle we did not start, in a world we did not make. We have been chosen to usher in either a new generation of hope or a new generation of terror.

U.S. AIR FORCE

My courage has been more severely tested when
I have spoken out against our excessive military
budget or the policy in Vietnam than it was when
I was flying combat missions as a pilot in
World War II.

Most of my close friends were killed in that
war. I vowed from the depth of my heart that if I
survived, I would devote the rest of my life to the
cause of peace. And no matter what else happens,
that is a pledge I am going to keep.

U.S. ARMY—
SSG HOWARD C. BREEDLOVE

WIDE WORLD

Our deepening involvement in Vietnam represents the most tragic diplomatic and moral failure in our national experience.

The mightiest nation in history—a nation with a glorious democratic tradition based on the dignity and brotherhood of man—is, with allegedly good motives, devastating an impoverished little state and ravishing the people whose freedom we would protect.

In the process we are sacrificing many of our bravest young men, wasting valuable resources, and threatening the peace of the world. We are being pulled step by step into a jungle quicksand that may claim our sons and the sons of Asia for years to come.

LIFE MAGAZINE—RONALD L. HAEBERLE

Congress must never again surrender its power under our constitutional system by permitting an ill-advised undeclared war of this kind.

In the name of humanity and all that is decent, let us end the bombardment of Indochina; let us bring our prisoners and our troops home; let us end the terrible waste and killings; let us do these things now, before we lose the soul of our nation.

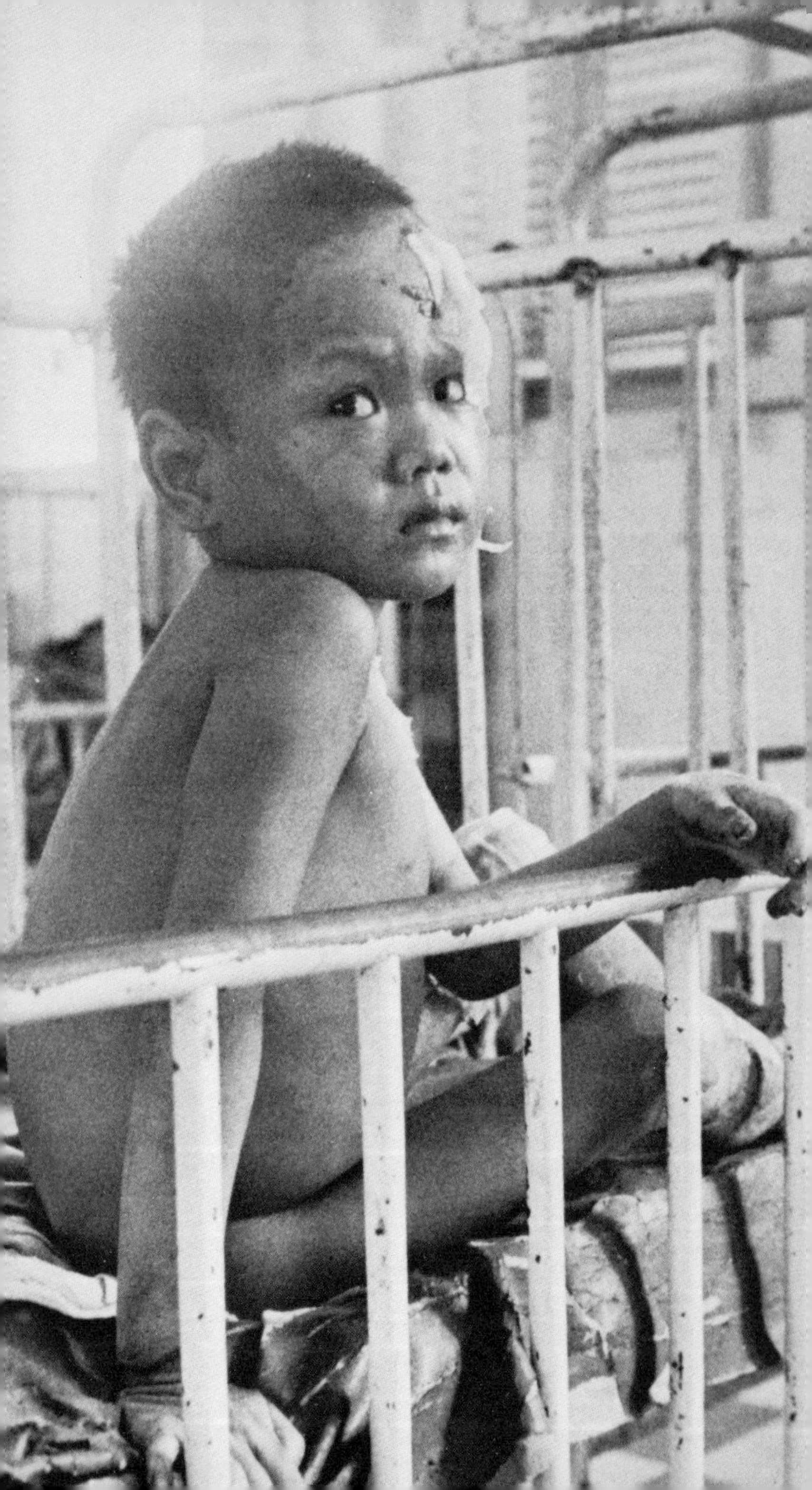

Little children with their faces blown off by *our* napalm . . . you could scarcely tell the child's face from the back of his head . . . people whose brown eyes reminded me of a wounded deer I once saw, as the hunters moved in.



JILL KREMENTZ

Communism is a force hostile to American ideals, but we do not meet its challenge by forcing an American solution on a people still in search of their own national identity.

After all the dead are counted—American and Vietnamese—and the countryside is laid waste, what will we then have accomplished?



U.S. ARMY—M/SGT AL CHANG

U.S. AIR FORCE

If my state, South Dakota, were to secede from
the union and become an independent country,
with its one hundred and sixty Minuteman missiles,
its Strategic Air Command Base, it would become
the third-ranking nuclear power in the world.

JILL KREMENTZ

Who really appointed us to play God for people elsewhere around the globe?

JILL KREMENTZ

When a major percentage of the public resources of our society is devoted to the accumulation of devastating weapons of war, the spirit of democracy suffers. When our laboratories and our universities and our scientists and our youth are caught up in war preparations, the spirit of free men is hampered.

WIDE WORLD

## The Economy and Employment

It will require a genuine commitment to put America to work . . . not on the business of war . . . not on the business of keeping corrupt foreign dictators in power . . . but on the business of building up America.

N.Y. POST—IKE VEIN

What does it do to our nation to invest annually more than half of our entire national budget in building the weapons of death, while neglecting the quality of our schools, our cities, and our lives?

I believe that to help the economy we must first help people.

N.Y. POST—ARTIE POMERANTZ

Americans don't mind paying taxes, they only want to know the system is fair—and today they know it isn't.

Taxation in any form must be based on ability to pay . . . not on convenience of collection.

We desperately need housing, schools, day-care centers, health care, new transit systems, anti-pollution devices, and environmental programs of many kinds.

There's enough work in this country for every man and woman who is capable of working if we set our values straight.



N.Y. POST

The Nixon Administration has a game plan. The main feature is to kick the American worker off the team.

Their plan for ending inflation is to make unemployment so high that no one can buy anything.

Their plan for ending unemployment is to make prices so high that it doesn't matter whether you work or not.



JILL KREMENTZ

I don't believe that the poor, our minority groups, or any other group of Americans really want a dole. What they desire is a recognition of their worth as individuals and their right to an equal opportunity.



JILL KREMENTZ

## Civil Rights

**I shall seek to call America home to those principles that gave us birth.**

WIDE WORLD

We do not serve America's interest by fighting so blindly to export freedom to Asia that we sacrifice it here at home. There is no interest in Southeast Asia that is great enough to justify silencing free speech and debate in America.

JILL KREMENTZ

I can say that our lives—black and white—were made better by his having lived.

WIDE WORLD

Liberty is not divisible. You cannot be free to support and not to oppose, to approve and not to criticize.

WIDE WORLD

I hope for the day when we do not need to specify that "Liberty and Justice for ALL" includes blacks, Chicanos, American Indians, women, homosexuals, or any other group. ALL means ALL.

N.Y. POST

Martin Luther King and James Meredith and Medgar Evers have without question moved the Negro's demand for full citizenship to the point of no return.

JILL KREMENTZ

I think if we can understand the spirit of 1776, we can better appreciate the rising expectations that are convulsing the American Negro community and the developing continents of the globe.

N.Y. POST—JERRY ENGEL

Thomas Paine from Bibliothèque National de Paris

Looking back over our history, it is remarkable how often we honor men who in their own time were viewed as dangerous dissenters.

VOTE

# Women

**Prejudice against women is the last socially accepted bigotry.**

JILL KREMENTZ

We must live up to the Constitution. Women have life, but they do not trully have freedom, and their pursuit of happiness is blocked at every turn, if they do not concede happiness to be limited to the "little woman" role.

N.Y. POST—VIC DeLUCIA

Never again should the question of war or peace be an all-male decision. Never again should our affairs of state be an all-male decision.

N.Y. POST—VIC DeLUCIA

I believe that Federal funds should not go to any institution that discriminates against women: not in admissions, not in hiring, not in promotion, not in salary.

As we limit our women, so do we limit our nation.



WIDE WORLD

WIDE WORLD

# Youth

**So my generation helped build a base for your generation. And now we have given you something that was not given to us—the right to vote. With it you can insure that our society will be better able than ever before to meet the needs of future generations.**

BUILd

Those of you who are young must serve our society in order to preserve what is as old as man himself: his quest for peace and freedom and dignity. And we do not despair. The tide of a new world is coming in.



JILL KREMENTZ

JILL KREMENTZ

The minds of our young people are our most precious resource.

Everywhere the praises of education are sung—everywhere, that is, except in the dry pages of the budget of the United States Government; those pages tell a very different story.

We must strive to see that every child—regardless of race or religion—receives the highest possible quality of education.

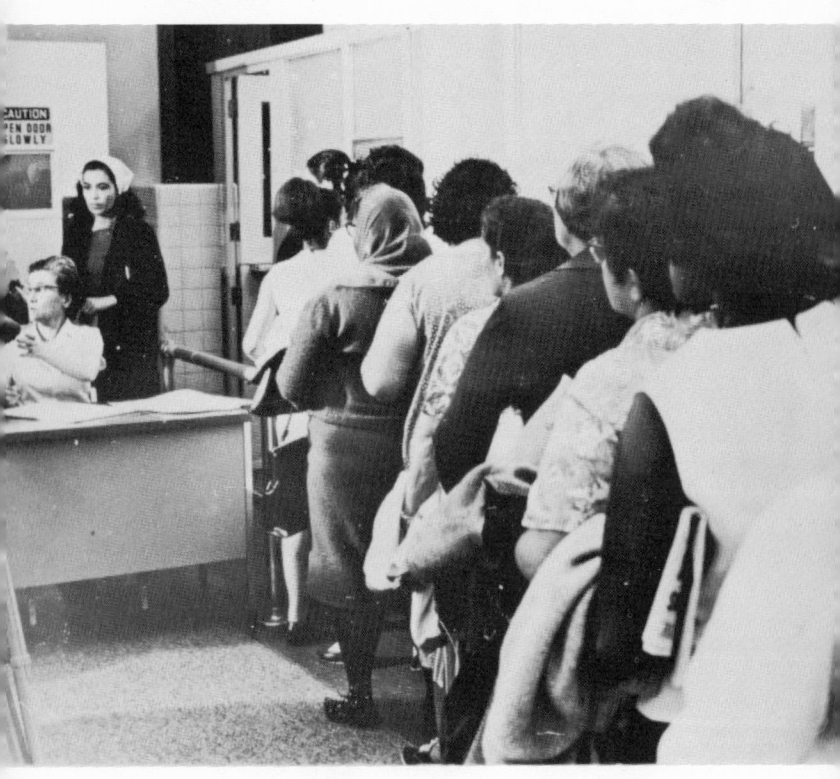


N.Y. POST—ARTIE POMERANTZ

## Senior Citizens

**Good health-care is the right of every American citizen.**

JILL KREMENTZ

The quality of any society can be measured by the manner in which it treats its older citizens.

JILL KREMENTZ

For too long, we have looked upon the rights of senior citizens as though they were privileges. In fact, it all boils down to one right—the right of survival—and I believe that the Federal Government must guarantee that right.

WIDE WORLD

In the world around us, I see this planet on a collision course between unchecked population growth and world hunger on a terrifying scale.

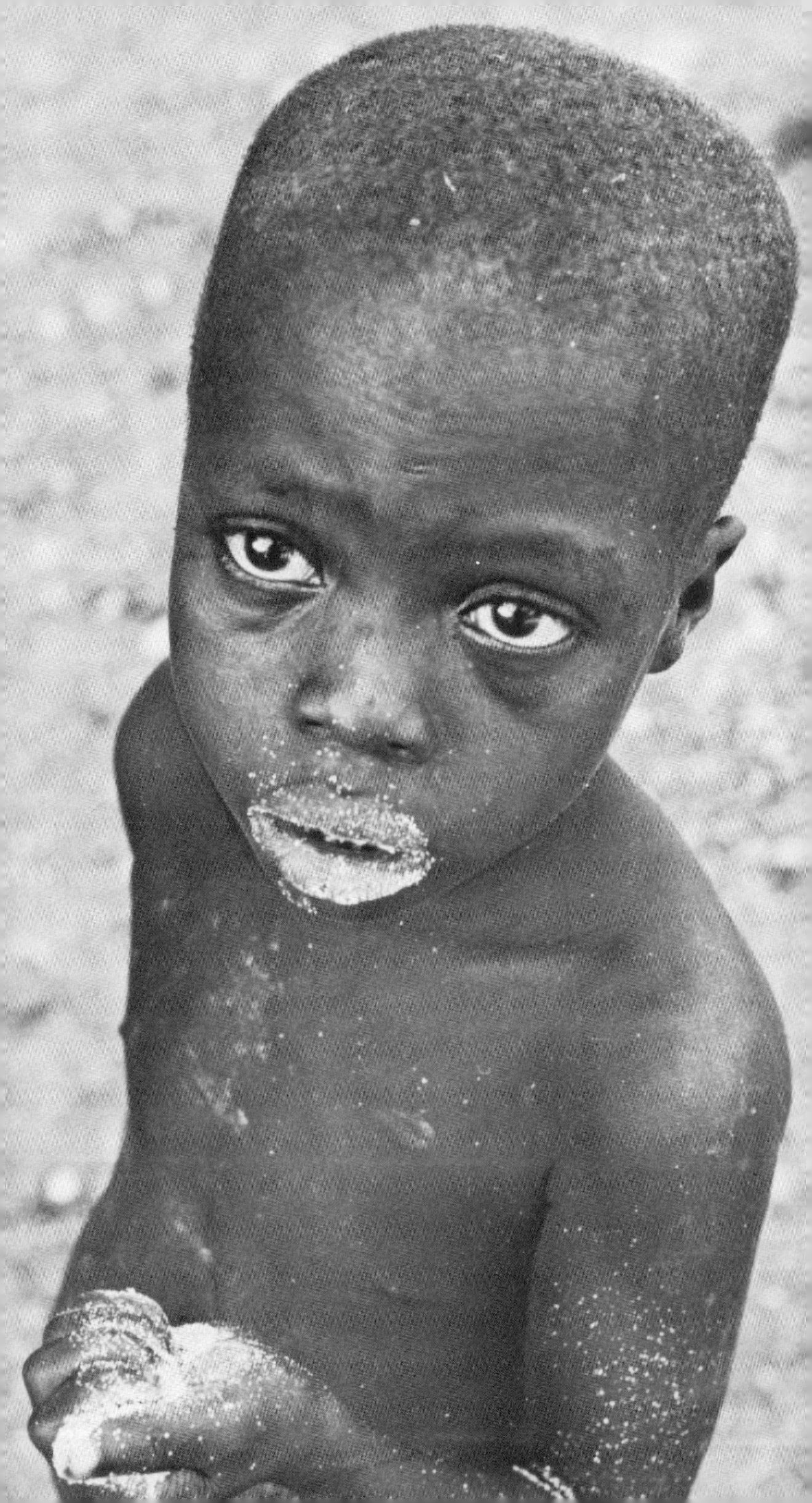

# Hunger

Four million children went to bed hungry again tonight; so did ten million adults. . . .

The Nixon Administration can't find the money to feed our people.

I can. And I will.

UNICEF

Hunger is the silent enemy. It is a thief in the night that steals away the children in ten thousand villages around the globe. While we Americans worry about overweight and reducing-pills, millions of our fellow human beings are fighting for survival.

NASA

WIDE WORLD

In spite of difficulties, a nation that can send a man to the moon can solve the problems of food production and distribution.

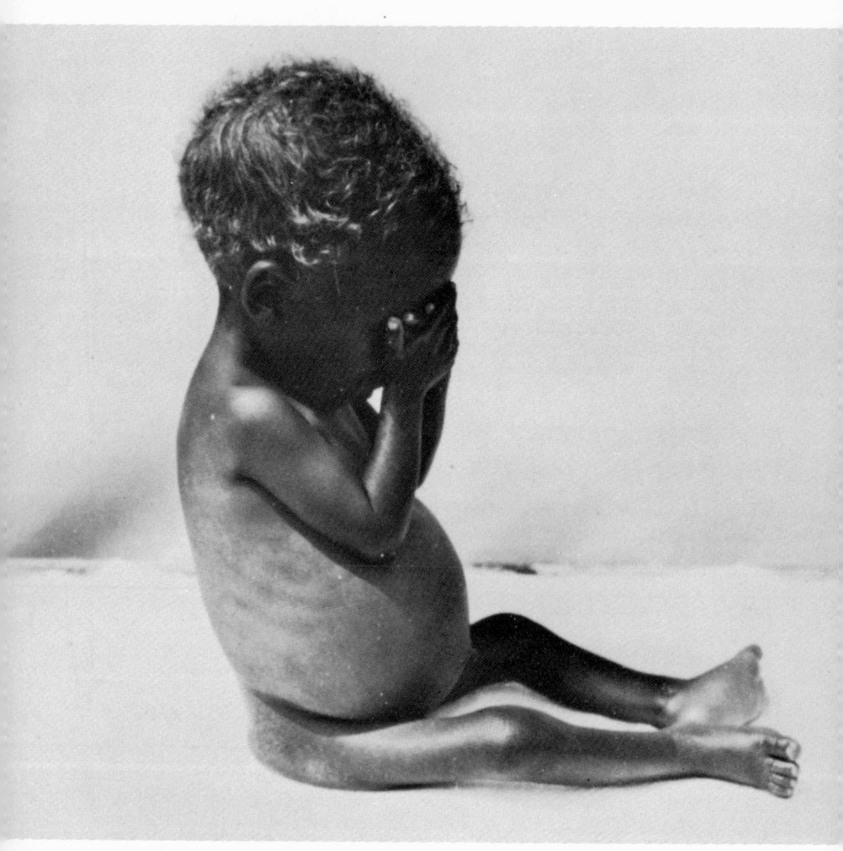

UNICEF PHOTO BY FAO

For one American to suffer from malnutrition is an affront to all Americans.

One can only guess at the price society pays for poverty and neglect; likewise it is not possible to appraise the dividends society receives from realizing the potential of one human life.

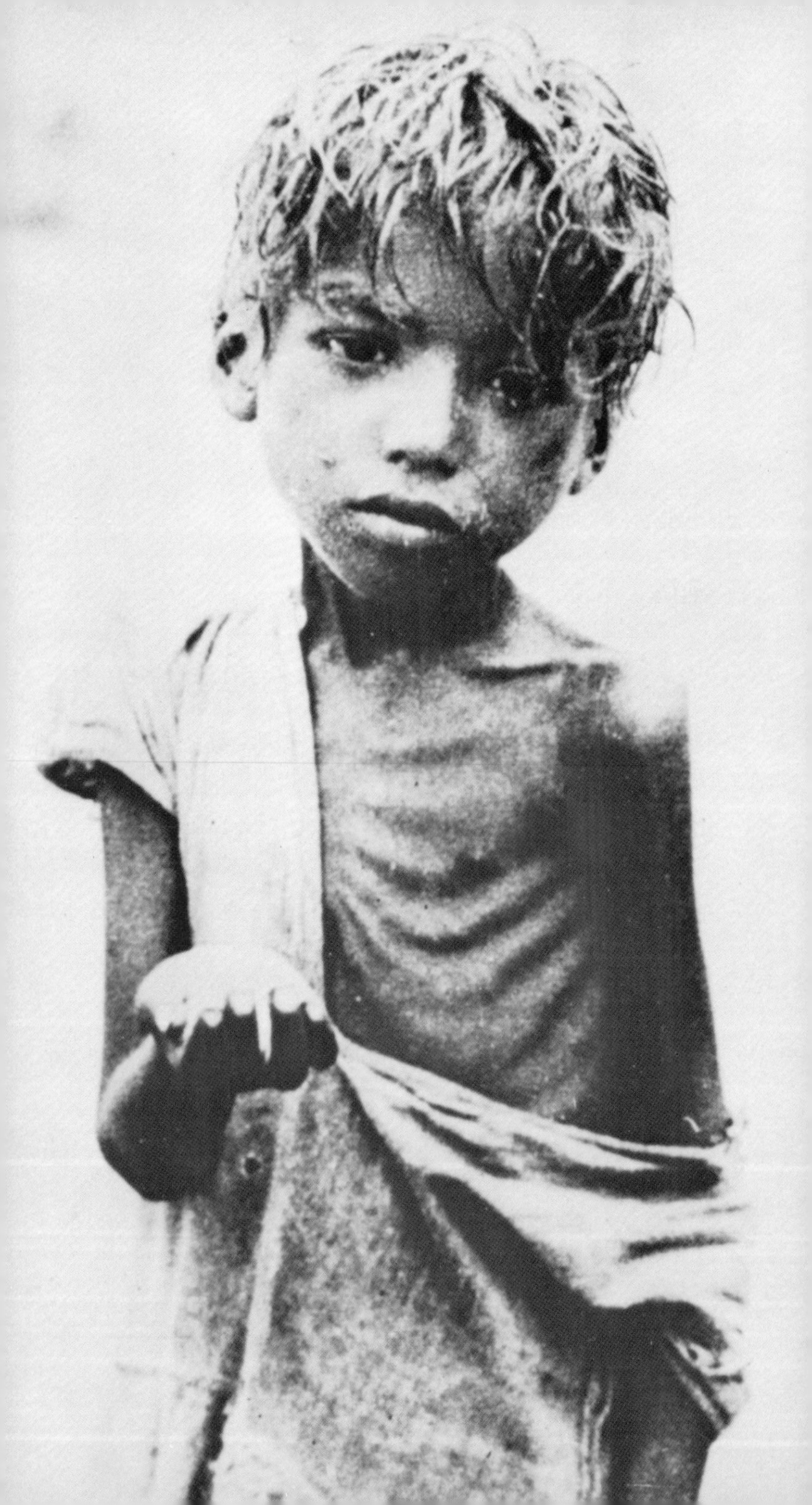

Solving the hunger problem will do more for peace around the globe than all the military weapons in our arsenal.



I.C.A.

C.P. WIREPHOTO

# Environment

**The prospect of a stagnant, polluted nation ranks with national defense, education, and health as essentials in our national life.**

U.S. FOREST SERVICE

Destruction of our environment may be the chief "spin-off" of all our technological innovation.

BLACK STAR—ALAN HAUN

We're not going to have another chance at replacing these God-given resources once they're destroyed.

We are threatening the very basis of life by upsetting the fragile ecological balance of man's environment.



WIDE WORLD

# Cities

Our cities constitute a precious heritage; they have been the historic centers of economic growth and cultural creativity. If they slowly die, or go up in flames, the whole American experiment fails too.



O.E.O.

Public housing should be scattered across the metropolis rather than concentrated in the inner city, and rewards should be offered for cooperative recreation and for air- and water-pollution programs.



O.E.O.

N.Y. POST—VERNON SHIBLA

What have we done for our cities?

JILL KREMENTZ

The Federal Government must commit itself to unifying city and suburbs in a common assault on metropolitan problems.

BLACK STAR—KOSTI RUOHOMAA

# Agriculture

**We face a choice between population stacked up in polluted, congested, crime-infested and job-poor cities, or a population spread out across the country, with room to live and breathe and prosper.**

BLACK STAR—RALPH CRANE

America has no greater need today than justice for rural America. A fair price for farm products has been and will continue to be my number one priority for rural America. Once that objective is achieved, rural America can begin to flourish.

The best protection we can have against soaring food prices is an adequate flow of credit for the family farmer.

BLACK STAR—HERBERT LANKS

Food for Americans is more vital than guns for Vietnam. Yet agriculture in America today has a lower priority than our massive expenditures for questionable ABM's, a lower priority than our forays into space, a lower priority than our handouts to the aerospace industry.

If the United States survives this critical period as a leader among nations, it will not be due to our weaponry but rather to the fact that we are still able to feed and clothe our people.

U.P.I. PHOTO

# REMARKS BY SENATOR GEORGE McGOVERN ACCEPTING THE DEMOCRATIC NOMINATION FOR THE PRESIDENCY OF THE UNITED STATES

## Miami Beach, Florida
## July 13, 1972

## "THIS IS THE TIME"

With a full heart, I accept your nomination.

My nomination is all the more precious in that it is the gift of the most open political process in our national history. It is the sweet harvest cultivated by tens of thousands of tireless volunteers—old and young—and funded by literally hundreds of thousands of small contributors. Those who lingered on the edge of despair a brief time ago have been brought into this campaign—heart, hand, head, and soul.

I have been the beneficiary of the most remarkable political organization in American history—an organization that gives dramatic proof to the power of love and to a faith that can move mountains. As Yeats put it, "Count where man's glory most begins and ends, and say, my glory was I had such friends."

This is a nomination of the people, and I hereby dedicate this campaign to the people.

And next January we will restore the government to the people. American politics will never be the same again.

We are entering a new period of important, hopeful change in America comparable to the political ferment released in the eras of Jefferson, Jackson, and Roosevelt.

I treasure this nomination especially because it comes after vigorous competition with the ablest men and women our party can offer.

My old and treasured friend and neighbor, Hubert Humphrey; that gracious and good man from Maine, Ed Muskie; a tough fighter for his beliefs, Scoop Jackson; a brave and spirited woman, Shirley Chisholm; a wise and powerful lawmaker from Arkansas, Wilbur Mills; the man from North Carolina who opened new vistas in education and public excellence, Terry Sanford; the leader who in 1968 combined the travail and the hope of the American spirit, Gene McCarthy.

I was as moved as all of you by the appearance at this convention of the governor of Alabama, George Wallace, whose votes in the primaries showed the depth of discontent in this country, and whose courage in the face of pain and adversity is the mark of a man of boundless will. We all despise the senseless act that disrupted his campaign. Governor, we pray for your speedy and full recovery, so you can stand up and speak out forcefully for all of those who see you as their champion.

In the months ahead, I covet the help of every Democrat and every Republican and independent who wants America to be the great and good land it can be.

This is going to be a national campaign carried to every part of the nation—North, South, East, and West. We are not conceding a single state to Richard Nixon. I want to say to my friend, Frank King, that Ohio may have passed a few times at this convention, but I'm not going to pass Ohio. Governor Gilligan, Ohio may be a little slow counting the votes, but when they come in this November, they are going to show a Democratic victory.

To anyone in this hall or beyond who doubts the ability of Democrats to join together in common cause, I say never underestimate the power of Richard Nixon to bring harmony to Democratic ranks. He is our unwitting unifier and the fundamental issue of this campaign. And all of us together are going to help him redeem the pledge he made ten years ago: Next year you won't have Richard Nixon to kick around anymore.

We have had our fury and our frustrations in these past months and at this convention.

Well, I frankly welcome the contrast with the smug, dull, and empty event which will take place here in Miami next month. We chose this struggle. We reformed our party and let the people in.

And we stand today not as a collection of backroom strategists, not as a tool of ITT or any other special interest, but as a direct reflection of the public will.

So let our opponents stand on the status quo, while we seek to refresh the American spirit.

Let the opposition collect their $10 million in secret money from the privileged. And let us find one million ordinary Americans who will contribute $25 each to this campaign—a McGovern "Million Member Club" with members who will expect not special favors for themselves, but a better land for us all.

In Scripture and in the music of our children we are told: "To everything there is a season, and a time to every purpose under heaven."

And for America, the time has come at last.

This is the time for truth, not falsehood.

In a democratic nation, no one likes to say that his inspiration came from secret arrangements behind closed doors. But in a sense that is how my candidacy began. I am here as your candidate tonight in large part because, during four administrations of both parties, a terrible war has been charted behind closed doors.

I want those doors opened, and I want that war closed. And I make these pledges above all others—the doors of government will be opened, and that brutal war will be closed.

Truth is a habit of integrity, not a strategy of politics. And if we nurture the habit of candor in this campaign, we will continue to be candid once we are in the White House. Let us say to Americans, as Woodrow Wilson said in his first campaign, "let me inside [the government] and I will tell you everything that is going on in there."

And this is a time not for death, but for life.

In 1968, Americans voted to bring our sons home from Vietnam in peace—and since then, twenty thousand have come home in coffins.

I have no secret plan for peace. I have a public plan.

As one whose heart has ached for ten years over the agony of Vietnam, I will halt the senseless bombing of Indochina on Inauguration Day.

There will be no more Asian children running ablaze from bombed-out schools.

There will be no more talk of bombing the dikes or the cities of the North.

Within ninety days of my inauguration, every American soldier and every American prisoner will be out of the jungle and out of their cells and back home in America where they belong.

And then let us resolve that never again will we shed the precious young blood of this nation to perpetuate an unrepresentative client abroad.

Let us choose life, not death. This is the time.

This is also the time to turn away from excessive preoccupation overseas to rebuilding our own nation.

America must be restored to her proper role in the world. But we can do that only through the recovery of confidence in ourselves. The greatest contribution America can make to our fellow mortals is to heal our own great but deeply troubled land. We must respond to that ancient command, "Physician, heal thyself."

It is necessary in an age of nuclear power and hostile ideologies that we be militarily strong. America must never become a second-rate nation. As one who has tasted the bitter fruits of our weakness before Pearl Harbor, 1941, I give you my sacred pledge that if I become president of the United States, America will keep its defenses alert and fully sufficient to meet any danger. We will do that not only for ourselves, but for those who deserve and need the shield of our strength—our old allies in Europe, and elsewhere, including the people of Israel, who will always have our help to hold their promised land.

Yet we know that for thirty years we have been so absorbed with fear and danger from abroad that we have permitted our own house to fall into disarray. We must now show that peace and prosperity can exist side by side—indeed, each now depends on the other.

National strength includes the credibility of our system in the eyes of our own people as well as the credibility of our deterrent in the eyes of others abroad. National security includes schools for our children as well as silos for our missiles, the health of our families as much as the size of our bombs, the safety of our streets and the condition of our cities and not just the engines of war. And if we someday choke on the pollution of our own air, there will be little consolation in leaving behind a dying continent ringed with steel.

Let us protect ourselves abroad and perfect ourselves at home.

This is the time.

And we must make this a time of justice and jobs for all.

For more than three years, we have tolerated stagnation and a rising level of joblessness, with more than five million of our best workers unemployed. Surely this is the most false and wasteful economics. Our deep need is not for idleness but for new housing and hospitals, for facilities to combat pollution and take us home from work, for products better able to compete on vigorous world markets.

The higest domestic priority of my administration will be to ensure that every American able to work has a job to do. This job guarantee will and must depend upon a reinvigorated private economy, freed at last from the uncertainties and burdens of war. But it is our commitment that whatever employment the private sector does not provide, the federal government will either stimulate or provide itself. Whatever it takes, this country is going back to work.

Americans cannot exist with most of our people working and paying taxes to support too many others mired in the demeaning, bureaucratic welfare system. Therefore, we intend to begin by putting millions back to work; and after this is done, we will assure to those unable to work an income sufficient to assure a decent life.

Beyond this, a program to put America back to work demands that work be properly rewarded. That means the end of a system of economic controls in which labor is depressed, but prices and corporate profits are the highest in history. It means a system of national health insurance, so that a worker can afford decent health care for himself and his family. It means real enforcement of the laws so that the drug racketeers are put behind bars for good and our streets are once again safe for our families.

Above all, honest work must be rewarded by a fair and just tax system. The tax system today does not reward hard work—it penalizes it. Inherited or invested wealth frequently multiplies itself while paying no taxes at all. But wages earned on the assembly line, or laying bricks, or picking fruit—these hard-earned dollars are taxed to the last penny. There is a depletion allowance for oil wells, but no allowance for the depletion of a man's body in years of toil.

The administration tells us that we should not discuss tax reform in an election year. They would prefer to keep all discussion of the tax code in closed committee rooms, where the administration, its powerful friends and their paid lobbyists, can turn every effort at reform into a new loophole for the rich. But an election year is the people's year to speak—and this year the people are going to ensure that the tax system is changed so that work is rewarded and so that those who derive the highest benefits will pay their fair share, rather than slipping through the loopholes at the expense of the rest of us.

So let us stand for justice and jobs, and against special privilege. This is the time.

We are not content with things as they are. We reject the view of those who say, "America—love it or leave it." We reply, "Let us change it so we can love it the more."

And this is the time. It is the time for this land to become again a witness to the world for what is noble and just in human affairs. It is the time to live more with faith and less with fear—with an abiding confidence that can sweep away the strongest barriers between us and teach us that we truly are brothers and sisters.

So join with me in this campaign, lend me your strength and your support, give me your voice—and together, we will call America home to the founding ideals that nourished us in the beginning.

From secrecy and deception in high places, come home, America.

From a conflict in Indochina which maims our ideals as well as our soldiers, come home, America.

From military spending so wasteful that it weakens our nation, come home, America.

From the entrenchment of special privilege and tax favoritism, come home, America.

From the waste of idle hands to the joy of useful labor, come home, America.

From the prejudice of race and sex, come home, America.

From the loneliness of the aging poor and the despair of the neglected sick, come home, America.

Come home to the affirmation that we have a dream.

Come home to the conviction that we can move our country forward.

Come home to the belief that we can seek a newer world.

And let us be joyful in that homecoming.

For,

*This land is your land,*
*This land is my land,*
*From California to the New York island,*
*From the Redwood Forest to the Gulfstream waters,*
*This land was made for you and me.*

May God grant us the wisdom to cherish this good land and to meet the great challenge that beckons us home.

BLACK STAR—FRED WARD

**GEORGE McGOVERN** was born in Avon, South Dakota, on July 19, 1922, the son of a Methodist clergyman. He graduated from Dakota Wesleyan University and earned his Ph.D. in History and government at Northwestern.

In World War II, Senator McGovern was the pilot of the B-24, "Dakota Queen." He flew 35 missions and was decorated with the Distinguished Flying Cross. He returned to serve as a professor at his Alma Mater.

In 1953, Senator McGovern became the executive secretary of the South Dakota Democratic Party. He served in the U.S. House of Representatives in 1957–1961. In January 1961, President Kennedy appointed him first director of the Food for Peace program and Special Assistant to the President.

He was elected to the Senate in 1962 and re-elected in 1968. He is Chairman of the Senate Select Committee on Nutrition and Human Needs and of the Senate Subcommittee on Indian Affairs. He is a member of the Committees on Agriculture and Interior.

Following the 1968 Democratic Convention, Senator McGovern was named Chairman of the Commission on Party Structure and Delegate Selection. In April 1970, the Commission laid down guidelines which ensured that the 1972 Convention would be the most open in history.

Senator McGovern is the author of three books: "War Against Want," 1964; Agricultural Thought in the Twentieth Century, 1967; and "A Time Of War/A Time Of Peace" 1968.

The Senator and his wife Eleanor have five children and two grandsons.